M000045845

THE US MILITARY:
IS THIS THE CAREER FOR YOU?

A guide to military enlistment

by Miguel A. Nieves

Copyright ©2019

All rights reserved, including the right to reproduce this book or portions thereof in any form.

ACKNOWLEDGMENTS

Although serving twenty-five years active duty in the Marine Corps required my own discipline, patience, time, and motivation, amongst many other things, to say I did it alone would be wrong. I am successful because of my family and friends.

A special thanks to a large cadre of uncles and aunts from whom I drew knowledge and strength. Over the years it has been great to have their guidance, advice, and friendship.

Uncle Efrain Andujar, you are the man! Funny, smart, and always ready to dish out great advice.

My late mother, Consuelo Nieves, words cannot begin to define what you accomplished in your lifetime as a mother and friend.

To my wife, Corinne, son, Miguel, and daughter, Carina, thank you for putting up with me. Is it time for another road trip?

I would like to thank all the Marines who helped me along the way. The Marine Corps practically raised me. I learned many lessons that to this day serve me well.

A special thanks to all my family members.

I am only successful because you all made me successful.

TABLE OF CONTENTS

CHAPTER 1

WHY WRITE THIS BOOK?

I have asked myself this question many times. Sometimes, when listening to coworkers in the break room or people in line at a coffee shop, I learn about the misconceptions people have about the military. I now work for the United States Postal Service, and although the Postal Service currently employs about 190,000 veterans, I am still surrounded by many people who don't know much about the military. They only know what they see on television shows and movies, or they piece together information they get from other, nonmilitary people. Most of the information they have is inaccurate. It has been quite a few years since I retired from the Marine Corps, however, I am still an insider; my last eleven years were in the recruiting field.

Over the years, family, friends, and neighbors have asked me about my experiences in the military. Sometimes they know someone who is thinking about joining and they send that young person to me. After listening to my responses, these young adults tell me I should write a book. They say they like my opinions and answers because my answers don't tell them whether to join or not; what I tell them simply provides them with the knowledge they need in order to make their own decision.

But what was I going to write? What did I have to say that would be interesting or useful to the reader? After mulling it over, I decided that this book should first and foremost be clear and to the point. It should be easy to follow and useful to those interested in learning about joining the military. I also decided that the goal of the book is to give you the most accurate and honest information about military recruiting and life in the military. I wanted the book to benefit anyone thinking about joining and their loved ones also. I wanted you to feel a little more educated about your decision. Let me also state that the purpose of this book is not to convince you to enlist or not. It is to educate you so you can take this information and add it to the information you gather online, at the recruiter's office, and from your friends and family, then put it all together and decide for yourself. Everyone likes to be told how right they are; when you are done reading this book you are going to be right. Right about a lot of things pertaining to military recruiting and how the process works for you, the applicant.

Last but not least, as you read, take notes of anything useful, and review those notes before meeting a recruiter for the first time. Don't disqualify yourself based on something you read in this book, because times and regulations for recruiting change. The more honest you are with your recruiter, the more time you will save and the better able the recruiter will be to determine your qualifications. Some disqualifications are not permanent, and a good recruiter will guide you in the right direction and tell you the truth.

CHAPTER 2

FOR PARENTS

This chapter takes you through the steps of the enlistment process. Up-to-date information can be learned directly from your kid's recruiter. So, let's get to it.

First, your child displays an interest in the military. This interest could come from movies, a family member, friends, toys, video games, television commercials, etc. There are inner and outer influences that impact a young adult and may get them thinking about joining the military. Honestly, some kids are born with that desire from the get-go; they are always exercising and will never accept any career path besides the military. I have met a few of these and still had to sit them down and explain the seriousness of their military obligations before enlisting them.

Once your kid decides to make contact with a military recruiter, he or she will be screened to determine if they meet the minimum qualifications. If a recruiter is doing their job properly, they are screening to disqualify. Yes, you read that correctly: The recruiter should be screening to disqualify your kid. This will save both your kid and the recruiter time.

The recruiter should ask questions to do with three major areas: education, police involvement, and physical condition.

Education

All applicants must be a high school graduate or a high school senior in good standing to graduate on time. Your kid has either already taken the Armed Service Vocational Aptitude Battery (ASVAB) test in school recently or is able to pass it easily. This is a three-hour test comparable to the Scholastic Achievement Test (SAT). With your child's consent, the recruiter will administer a pretest in the recruiter's office to determine if your kid has the aptitude to pass the ASVAB. If your kid passes the pretest, they will be invited to take the ASVAB, free of charge. This test is sometimes taken at a designated testing site or at a Military Entrance Processing Station (MEPS). Your kid needs to understand that agreeing to take the ASVAB with a recruiter is done only with a commitment to enlist. This is part of the recruitment processing chain. The better your kid scores on the ASVAB test, the more programs and bonuses (if available) the recruiter can offer with a contract for enlistment.

A young applicant who has applied themselves during their middle school and high school years will generally do well on the ASVAB. After an applicant has passed the ASVAB, they can discuss with their recruiter what their scores qualify them for. Some high schools administer the ASVAB to their eleventh- and twelfth-grade students. If the score is high and not older than two years, it can be used for enlistment.

There are books available for purchase to help you learn what is in the ASVAB; they also contain sample tests for your kid to practice. There are also a number of free apps that takes no longer than three minutes to install on a cell phone. The apps provide a great tool for the user to practice questions on all ASVAB subjects, and includes one or more practice tests.

It has been my experience that most applicants who initially fail the ASVAB are able to pass it on a subsequent attempt after taking a few classes in math and English at a local community college. Some of my applicants hired math and English tutors to get the passing grade, which is absolutely legal and acceptable.

If your child scores a perfect or near-perfect score on the ASVAB, they should be given the opportunity to speak with an officer selection officer (known as an OSO in the Marine Corps). This officer will speak with your child to learn if they are interested in a military career as an officer, as opposed to the enlisted ranks.

Likewise, if your kid has completed some college or is a college graduate, they need to ensure the recruiter is informed of this. This also may lead to an enlistment in the officer ranks.

Let me give you a scenario that military recruiters on occasion run into. A high school senior with below-average grades scores high on their school-administered ASVAB, or scores high in their pretest at the recruiter's office. Although they are prequalified for enlistment into the delayed entry program, the recruiter will not enlist them until the student has shown improvement in their grades. The goal of any recruiter is to enlist those who are prequalified, which includes graduating on time with your senior class.

Police Involvement

Your kid is going to be asked questions pertaining to any possible police involvement. The purpose of these questions is not to offend anyone but to ensure that only the qualified get into our military ranks. So, what type of police involvement do recruiters want to know about? Everything. If your child had a petty theft charge at age eleven, we want to know about it. It wouldn't necessarily disqualify them. Parents, tell your kid to be honest with the recruiter. We have moral waivers to forgive a person for most past violations of the law and that allow them to move forward with their military future.

Some more serious disclosures require that your kid show a history of improvement. Here is an example: Say your kid had a charge of grand theft auto at age sixteen. He managed to graduate high school by studying at night. He then continued pursuing higher education and earned an associate degree and is currently taking classes full time toward a bachelor's. Plus, since the age of sixteen he hasn't had any police involvement. Today he is twenty-one years old and wants to enlist. Because he has demonstrated a willingness to improve his life, the recruiter's commanding officer may be able to grant him a moral waiver for enlistment. Be aware that every case is different and will be judged on its own merits. The different branches of the services all handle police involvement and moral waivers in their own way.

I would recommend that when the recruiter starts asking questions about police involvement, you (the parent) step out of the office. In my experience, applicants do not disclose everything when their parents are present.

The recruiter will ask your child about any type of legal and illegal drug use, whether or not police were involved. We need to know about any drugs your kid has used. The use of illegal drugs is not tolerated in the military. Testing positive for illegal drug use during the medical exam at MEPS is a disqualifier. While in the military, my fellow Marines and I were always subject to random urinalysis drug tests. The tests didn't bother me; I loved the idea of being surrounded by people who were drug free.

The policy on enlisting someone with former drug use or police involvement varies between the branches of the military. What one service may forgive and give your child a moral waiver for, another service may deem them disqualified.

At the time of writing, about eleven states have legalized marijuana. On the federal level, please know that your child can't enlist while being a marijuana user.

Physical Condition

The military recruiter is going to ask your child about any physical ailments, conditions, hospital visits, etc. What the recruiter is trying to do is ensure that your kid doesn't have any permanent or temporary physical disqualifications.

Again, it is important that your kid is honest with the recruiter. The recruiter will also do a height and weight measurement at the office, just like a doctor would. This height and weight measurement are used to determine your child's body mass index (BMI). BMI is nothing more than a measure of healthy versus unhealthy weight. Afterward, a recruiter may ask for medical documentation. Some applicants will be told they are overweight and don't qualify to enlist. Weight standards are in place for two reasons: 1) for the safety of your child so they will be less susceptible to injuries during training, and 2) for performance; when a Marine, soldier, sailor, or airman is in excellent physical condition, they can perform their assigned duties safely.

Once your kid has been screened on all three categories and found to be prequalified, they will be given a complete presentation on enlistment processing and military benefits. The length of this interview can be as short as thirty minutes or as long as a couple of hours, depending on the questions or concerns that the recruiter wants to address.

As a recruiter I ran into many scenarios during interviews. Some parents wanted to sit in on the prescreening and interview. Others wanted to wait in the office until it was over. Some just weren't interested and basically gave the kid a ride to and from the office. On a side note, a recruiter has a government-issued car to transport your child to and from the office free of charge. The recruiter is not allowed to transport anyone other than applicants in the car. So, parents, don't take it personally when the recruiter tells you he can only transport your child.

I always encouraged parents to sit in on the interview and hold all their questions until the end. When I was finished with the interview but before I asked the applicant if they were moving forward with enlistment, I asked parents for their questions or input.

If an applicant decided not to move forward with enlistment, either because they were shopping around with different branches of the military or were unsure about the commitment, I would simply ask permission to stay in touch.

I would continue to address any questions or concerns when I ran into these students in school.

If your kid decides to go ahead with the process and enlist, things will move forward in this order: The applicant will sign consent to a police check, juvenile police check, traffic check (check driving record), and, if still in high school, a check of school grades and status. If an applicant is a minor of seventeen years old, these checks can only be made with parental consent. This includes enlistment. Regardless of age, you will find that recruiters want the parents' blessing before moving forward with the young person's enlistment.

Next, your kid will be scheduled to take the ASVAB, which either happens that same day or the next day. The recruiter will normally pick up your kid in a government car and take them to the test site.

Once your child has taken the ASVAB, the recruiter will discuss the results of the test with them. The ASVAB test comprises ten sections and results in a few scores. The higher your child scores in some areas, the more military occupational specialties (MOS) they may qualify for. At the time of the ASVAB test, there might be some college bonuses, special programs, and deals available to your kid based on their ASVAB results.

For instance, let's say your kid's ASVAB scores qualifies them for an aviation mechanic program that they are interested in. At the same time there is also a deal whereby if your child enlists for a minimum of six years, they get a college fund of $50,000 to use in conjunction with their Montgomery GI Bill in the future.

Sometimes the military has enlistment bonuses, so don't be afraid to ask if any are available. Some bonuses require certain scores on the ASVAB while others require a certain length of enlistment. Some bonuses are for a specific field, such as a musician for the military band.

Remember that times change, and programs and opportunities change. The recruiter can only promise what is available at the time and what your child qualifies for.

After taking the ASVAB and coming to an agreement with the recruiter on what your child is signing up for, the next steps are the physical exam and enlistment. The recruiter will pick up your kid on the agreed day and take them to the MEPS. When your kid passes the physical exam and swears in to a military enlistment they will then be picked up by the recruiter to finalize the enlistment paperwork and agree on a ship date to boot camp. Your kid must know exactly which program, length of enlistment, and bonuses (if any) were awarded to them before they depart for boot camp. I believe that a commitment to serve our country from young adults should come with a commitment from their recruiter to provide them with an honest contract agreed upon by all parties involved.

Some applicants specifically want to join the military's special forces, such as the Navy Seals, Marine Recon, Army Rangers, or Green Berets. Applicants have to understand that these fields require exceptional qualifications and test results. A recruiter will give your child up-to-date information on what they need to do to earn a spot in a special forces team.

If your kid is a high school senior, they will be shipping to boot camp directly after graduation. In the meantime, they are in the delayed entry program. If your kid is a high school graduate, they will ship out based on the recruiter's availability dates.

Now that your kid has enlisted and is awaiting shipment to boot camp, it is critically important that they immediately start getting into good physical shape. Passing the medical exam at MEPS means your kid is cleared for military service. Now they must begin to *slowly* improve their physical condition by starting to *safely exercise*. This includes learning how to drink water. Yes, you read that correctly: learning how to drink water. Most young adults don't drink water or don't drink enough and are instead drinking soda or other drinks. The recruiter will provide the applicant with information related to boot camp and what they should learn before arriving for training. Some applicants will have a two-month wait, while others can wait for ten months. The maximum amount of time an applicant can be in the delayed entry program is one year.

With today's technology, parents have easy access to their kid's recruiter to ask questions and have any concerns addressed. In my opinion, it doesn't matter if your kid is seventeen or twenty-eight years old. They will always be your kid.

As a recruiter I always attempted to make sure the parents of all my applicants were both informed and involved in their kid's enlistment. I wanted to make sure they understood both the process and what their kids were signing on for.

Parents, I want to leave you with this. Upon graduating high school your child has three choices: higher education, joining the work force, or joining the military. Listen to them and provide them with leadership and guidance. We live in challenging times and the decision they make will affect them for the rest of their lives. I truly wish you all only the best.

CHAPTER 3

MOTIVATIONS FOR JOINING THE MILITARY

The first question you have to ask yourself is; why do you want to join the military? I have learned over the years that people from all walks of life join for many different reasons. And most times the reason for joining will evolve. You may have initially joined for one reason and then you find yourself staying and reenlisting for another reason altogether.

I have met many Marines who did one enlistment and then moved on to different occupations. Some save their money and attend as much college as possible before moving on. Some waste their time during their one enlistment complaining about everything and everyone, including their recruiters. They come in broke and leave broke with nothing to show for their one and only enlistment, but it's not their fault; it's everybody else's fault. I told you I would tell you the truth in this book, and yes, I did meet people that complained all the time and still reenlisted. Please don't ask me why they stayed; there was no draft at that time in our country.

I first joined because I was the eldest of six children and wanted to do something challenging right after high school, be the leader of the pack, if you will. Although I believe that, subconsciously, I also didn't like being a financial burden on my mother, who was raising us alone. As time passed with new travel and living abroad, I got to really enjoy the life and reenlisted after each contract. Most of my reenlistment contracts were for four years. I had one six-year reenlistment that came with a reenlistment bonus. The longer I stayed in the Marine Corps, the more training and experiences I received.

After I completed ten years, I recalled conversations I had with my friend and neighbor back home, Mr. Parker, about earning a retirement. I decided at that moment that I was in for the long haul and reenlisted again. No one else was offering a retirement with a minimum of only twenty years of work.

As a young Hispanic male in 1979 I wasn't groomed for attending college. No one in my family or school environment ever talked to me about college. High schools at that time in our country were conducting vocational training and preparing us for the workforce. I was in the electrical program in high school, so naturally my electronics information (EL) score on the Armed Service Vocational Aptitude Battery Test (ASVAB) was high.

Today, as when I was graduating high school, young adults still have one of three choices: they can join the workforce, join the military, or go to college. I didn't see myself going to college with no money and no real idea of what college could do for me, and I knew that the workforce was not going to hire me with just a high school diploma and a bit of training but no experience.

In the middle of my eleventh-grade year, my family moved

from Brooklyn, New York to Trenton, New Jersey. In my new neighborhood I met Mr. Parker. One day I asked him why he didn't work. I was paying attention and had noticed that everyone else was going to school or to work. But Mr. Parker was always home, tinkering around fixing cars. He explained that he had retired from the army. As a seventeen-year-old, I was naturally curious about retirement and how to get there. Mr. Parker and I became good friends, and he told me all about his experiences in the military—except Vietnam; we didn't go there. I quickly realized that was a subject he didn't want to discuss. Over the years Mr. Parker became one of my role models; he was someone I could talk to and someone who could listen to me. In the back of my head I stored that idea of early retirement; it interested me.

When my friend and high school classmate told me about how he had enlisted in the Marine Corps, I was somewhat interested. He introduced me to his recruiter, and I watched a boot camp video and learned about the challenges of life in the Marine Corps. I liked the idea of a challenge and travelling to places I had never been. I enlisted in the Z4 Mechanical-Electrical program at the time. And my friend got a stripe (promotion) upon graduating from boot camp for referring people that enlisted, me being one of them. I knew this and kind of liked the idea that my enlistment would help my friend.

I will truthfully tell you that military life is not for everyone. The military, regardless of branch, is something you should really look into carefully before committing to it.

Talk to people who have served. Friends and family members

are going to be honest with you about their personal experiences. Learn as much as you can and take notes. Some people are motivated to join, and some are dissuaded from joining for various reasons. No two people will have the exact same military experience. What may motivate you to stay in the military may very well convince someone else that the military is not for them.

I wrote a short note to some friends and family members and asked them to answer a few questions about their military experience. I include them here so you can read for yourself how different everyone is in their responses.

This is the note I sent them:

> I am writing a book about military recruiting and the process for both the applicants and their parents. While writing the book I wrote about how I decided to join and how that decision evolved as I continued to reenlist. I thought it would be a good idea to include quotes from friends and family members that also served. Here are a few questions that I am asking you to answer to help me in this endeavor. Thank you.

Walter E. Chancay Jr., US Marine

a. How did you come up with the idea to enlist in the military?

My childhood and adolescent years were a time of angst, mainly because I was growing up in a single-parent household and my mother was the sole provider for our family. I can certainly expound on how all of the challenges that I faced during the early stages of my human development were the driving force of my decision later in life, but I'll narrow the reasons down to the hardships of living in poverty and the limited resources of basic human needs.

By the time that I was a senior in high school, my family had moved a total of eight times, and this caused a lot of instability and insecurity in my life. I wasn't very confident in myself, mainly because I lacked the paternal and, in some ways, maternal support. Academically I wasn't doing very well in school, in fact, when I was enrolling in my fourth different high school I learned that I would not graduate on time and that the only way that I would possibly be able to walk with my graduating class was if I went to day and night school all year long. For the first time in my life I felt like a failure and really cared about what that would mean. I decided to take on the challenge of going to day and night school in order to graduate on time. Towards the end of my first semester as a senior I was doing well in both day and night school and started to feel a sense of accomplishment. I felt that I would be able to continue to do everything I needed to do in order to graduate on time. But I started to develop a fear of what would come next. I asked myself what would I do with my life after high school? I knew deep down inside that I wanted more for myself and my family. I understood that financially my mother would not be able to put me through college, and my grades were not where they needed to be to qualify for any type of scholarship; my options were limited.

One day while watching an NBA game on television I saw a Navy Seal commercial and it captured my attention. I sought out a Navy Recruiter at my high school and scheduled to meet him at the library during lunch time. My first impression of the recruiter was not what I had expected, nor what the commercial had advertised, which completely brought my level of interest down. Not to mention that the recruiter never followed up with me like he said he would do. For a moment in time my idea of finding out more information about the Navy faded away. That same week, a classmate learned about my interest in the Navy and asked if I had ever thought about the Marines as an option. My response was no. He asked if I would like to meet his recruiter to find out more information, and I told him that I had no transportation to get there or get back home. If he was willing to take me to his recruiter and then get me back home, I would be willing to go to the recruiting station. We agreed on a date and off we went.

My first impression of the Marine recruiter was excellent. Not only was his uniform sharp and neatly pressed, the man looked like a WWF wrestler, and on top of all that the first thing he asked me was, "What makes you think you have what it takes to be a Marine?" Whoa!! Challenge accepted. I was a kid from Brooklyn, NY with a chip on his shoulder already, so yeah, why not. That day I made the decision that what I was looking for in life was a challenge, a feeling of belonging to a family, being part of something that was bigger than my own insecurities. It all just poured out that day.

b. What was the most difficult thing or event you had to cope with during your first enlistment and why?

The most difficult thing that I had to cope with during my first enlistment was growing up. I was literally seventeen years old the first six months of my Marine Corps career, but now I had more disposable cash than I had ever had in my lifetime thus far. After leaving boot camp I felt that I was ready for the next challenge, and I silently hungered for the opportunity to be distinguished because I had missed my opportunity during boot camp. Next stop was Marine Combat Training. I excelled, and for the first time I started to develop more confidence in my true potential because I had people who believed in me and were providing me with direction on how to be better. Leaving MCT I was meritoriously promoted, and oh did it feel great!!

My downfall. During Camp Guard in Camp Lejeune, NC I was slated for a 0100 post, however, due to a lack of judgment on my part I chose to go out in town with friends, even though I had direct orders for on-base liberty only. I went off base anyway. My decision caused me to not be at my appointed place of duty when I was supposed to be there, and subsequently caused my leaders to question my judgment. Because I had been meritoriously promoted during MCT, my leaders decided that they would give me a second chance to prove my worth. I will never forget my NCO and SNCO who believed in me even after I had failed them. They could have certainly handled the situation differently and left a permanent blemish on my young career that ultimately would have affected the possibilities of reenlisting.

c. What was the easiest thing or event you coped with during your first enlistment and why?

I would have to say that the easiest thing that I was able to cope with was being away from my family, especially my mother, since up to that point we had always been together. My first duty station was in Cherry Point, NC, which was just ten hours south of my home state. During my first enlistment I found myself taking many road trips up to New York to visit my family, which made the transition from civilian to military much easier.

d. If you met a young adult today who was interested in joining the US military and you had a few minutes of their attention, what words of wisdom or advice would you give them?

Proper preparation prevents poor performance. Conduct as much research as possible to ensure you are making a well-educated and informed decision, consult with your family and loved ones on your decision, but finalize your decision on the basis of what is important to you and only you. Take into consideration what your short-term, mid-term, and long-term goals are, and determine if the service that you are considering joining has the organizational values that align with your desired end-state. Put yourself in a position where you have greater options, especially as it pertains to the different occupational specialties the military has to offer. Think about life after service, and consider if the skill that you will learn in service will be one that will make you competitive and marketable in a nation that is continuing to develop. The intangible skills and characteristics that will be instilled in you during your time of service will serve you well, however, you still need a workforce skill or trade that will be in demand if you want to continue to work.

e. How long did you serve and in what branch?

Twenty years, United States Marine Corps.

f. If you had to do it all over, what would you have done differently while serving in the military, if anything?

I would have taken advantage of the many different benefits that are available to every service member while on active duty. For example, I would use the Tuition Assistance Program to earn a post-secondary education, and then I would consider a Commissioning program.

I would have invested in the Thrift Savings Plan from the time that I was eligible, all the way up to retirement.

I would have signed up for the apprenticeship program and received certifications on human resources and counseling.

I would have been a Drill Instructor first then have gone back to the Fleet Marine Force, became a recruiter second, and 8412 career recruiter last.

g. What do you do now for a living?

I am finishing my master's degree in Business Administration, with an emphasis in Marketing.

h. In what city do you reside?

I reside in Temecula, CA, which is one hour north of

San Diego and an hour and a half south of Los Angeles.

Miguel,

Thank you for allowing me to share a little bit of my life story for your book. I look forward to reading it in the future.

Your friend,

Walter E. Chancay Jr. (Junior)

Eduardo Santos, US Marine

a. How did you come up with the idea to enlist in the military?

I took the ASVAB test during my junior year in high school. A couple of weeks later, my recruiter (Nieves) contacted me. At this point of my life, I had only lived in the United States for approximately five years and I was not aware that the military was an option for me. I did not have many post–high school aspirations; I was just going with the flow of mediocrity. Nieves introduced me to the idea of becoming a US Marine. He talked to me about the benefits without hyperbole and talked frankly about the hardships. I admit that at first I was hesitant to join due to my peers' (and my) misguided ideas about the military. However, Nieves successfully established a trusting relationship with me and more importantly with my mother; he managed to get her blessing and I was off to famous Parris Island.

The decision to join the Marine Corps was the catalyst to my professional and personal success. The Marine Corps has a history of turning lackluster youths (such as me) to honorable, courageous, disciplined, and strong-minded individuals. The qualities that the Marine Corps instilled deep within me have been the anchor that has allowed me to enjoy a long and successful career as a Special Agent in the US Foreign Service.

b. What was the most difficult thing or event you had to cope with during your first enlistment and why?

The first four weeks of boot camp. During this time, I was adjusting to the transition from my comfortable life as a high school student to the shocking reality of Marine Corps boot camp. This was a tough pill to swallow for even the toughest kids in my platoon. However, after I accepted my reality, the rest of boot camp was easy and actually kind of fun.

c. What was the easiest thing or event you coped with during your first enlistment and why?

I found that the easiest thing for me was the day-to-day life in my unit. Once I completed all my training, was assigned to my unit, and when I was no longer considered—as the Marines love to say—"the F-ing New Guy" (FNG), I found that the daily life as a Marine was not bad at all. I worked from nine to five with an excellent group of colleagues. After work, we were free to do as we pleased. I was lucky enough to be stationed in Hawaii. We had a beach on base, many gyms, swimming pools, and all the food you can eat (for free) at the cafeteria. In addition, several colleges had established satellite offices on base and offered college classes in the evenings. The Marine Corps paid 100 percent of my college tuition while I was on active duty and I was able to finish most of my bachelor's degree during my enlistment.

d. If you met a young adult today who was interested in joining the US military and you had a few minutes of their attention, what words of wisdom or advice would you give them?

Young man/lady, these are the benefits you get when you join the military:

World class physical and technical training, a job, decent pay, free housing, free food, free college, free travel, free health care, free gyms, access to military bases worldwide, a top-of-the-line retirement account, and veteran's preference for a federal government job. These are all great benefits that no other entity or private enterprise that I'm aware of offers a young adult fresh out of high school. However, for me, the most important benefits the military offers are the intangible ones that you can only obtain by experiencing, embracing, and overcoming physical and mental suffering. Intangibles, like mental toughness, the ability to deal with stress, self-confidence, courage, and many more are the foundation to a successful and satisfying life.

e. How long did you serve and in what branch?

Four years in the United States Marine Corps

f. If you had to do it all over, what would you have done differently while serving in the military, if anything?

I would not change anything. I made lots of mistakes, but the lessons learned from those mistakes allowed me to grow as a Marine and as a human being.

g. What do you do now for a living?

I am a Special Agent (Criminal Investigator) for the US Federal Government.

h. In what city do you reside?

I am presently working overseas in Pretoria, South Africa.

Juan Pinzon, US Marine

a. How did you come up with the idea to enlist in the military?

To this day, I still cannot remember why I became interested in the Marines. I have no prior military people in my family, and I did not know any active duty service member at the time. I just knew that the Marines are considered to be the best, the toughest branch, and that's what I decided to look into.

b. What was the most difficult thing or event you had to cope with during your first enlistment and why?

I would say that the most difficult thing was the big learning curve that I had to get used to during my first couple of years. The Marine Corps trains you well and screens you to be a leader, but there are many factors, often situation dependent. I did not have any family in the military and did not go through any sort of NROTC program, so Officer Candidate School (OCS) and The Basic School (TBS) were my first taste of the military. I had to adapt quickly and learn every day, everything including but not limited to administrative processes, terminology, command hierarchy, standard operating procedures, billet responsibilities, and staff relationships. Even to this day I continue learning and understand that every billet, command, and location is different.

c. What was the easiest thing or event you coped with during your first enlistment and why?

The Basic School (TBS) was one of the easiest events that I experienced. It was six long and hard months with a lot of physical and mental tests, injuries, long nights, and a lot to learn. However, it was easy because of the people I surrounded myself with, who had my back during those six months, and who are still great friends to this day. TBS makes you go through stressful moments and various events with the same people for six months. I very quickly identified those around me who had a similar mindset, who were optimistic and unselfish. Having people like this around me made TBS easy for all of us; we had fun during the tough moments and pushed each other to better ourselves. I have always believed that whether I enjoy a job or event has little to do with the location or the job itself. Rather, it is determined by the job environment and the people I interact with every day, whether it is my peers, boss, or subordinate Marines. It is the people that make each day enjoyable and who teach me something new every day.

d. If you met a young adult today who was interested in joining the US military and you had a few minutes of their attention, what words of wisdom or advice would you give them?

I would tell him/her that regardless of what they decide or are chosen to do in the military, he/she will have many opportunities to grow. That the military will make you a better person and instill self-discipline and confidence. Through the military, he/she will have to opportunity to see and experience many great things, learn, and improve themselves. The military has all these options and opportunities, but that it is up to the individual to stay hungry and have the drive and initiative to improve and seek them out. Through the military, it is likely that you will travel many places and meet people from all over the world and cultural backgrounds, so it is important to keep an open mind. I would tell them that the military has many rewards and life experiences whether you do it for four years or twenty. Most importantly, I would tell them to be humble and respect others, regardless of rank or experience, as human relationships are very important whether you are military or civilian.

e. How long did you serve and in what branch?

I am an active duty Marine for six years.

f. If you had to do it all over, what would you have done differently while serving in the military, if anything?

I am happy with where my career is at the moment. There are things that I have learned and ways in which I have changed that I wish I would have applied earlier in life. The discipline and constant desire for self-improvement that I have now would have opened many doors and made me a better person and Marine if I had these qualities when I was in high school and college. That is not to say that I was not driven or disciplined then, but I am definitely a different person and have a different mindset than I did back then. I cannot change the past, but I can share what I have learned and instill those qualities in my Marines, peers, kids, and everyone with whom I come in contact.

g. What do you do now for a living?

I am active duty military and just executed a Permanent Change of Station (PCS) for the third time.

h. In what city do you reside?

I live onboard Marine Corps Base, Hawaii.

Arthur Frederickson, US Navy

a. How did you come up with the idea to enlist in the military?

Where I came from, good employment opportunities were slim and I had no money for college. The military was a good prospect.

b. What was the most difficult thing or event you had to cope with during your first enlistment and why?

Being away from home for the first time on my own. I left everything and everyone I knew behind.

c. What was the easiest thing or event you coped with during your first enlistment and why?

Being at sea. I love the ocean. You also have the same basic routine each day.

d. If you met a young adult today who was interested in joining the US military and you had a few minutes of their attention, what words of wisdom or advice would you give them?

Look at all your options. The military life is not for everyone. Try and choose the branch and job that will help train you for the career you want to pursue after you get out, either after your first enlistment or after twenty-plus years.

e. How long did you serve and in what branch?

US Navy, twenty-three years.

f. If you had to do it all over, what would you have done differently while serving in the military, if anything?

Get a college degree using the GI bill.

g. What do you do now for a living?

Letter Carrier for the US Postal Service.

h. In what city do you reside?

South Florida.

Juan Dabdub, US Marine

a. How did you come up with the idea to enlist in the military?

Well, since before I even thought about coming to this country, I always heard about every other branch but the Marines, and I don't know why. I'm the first one in all my family to join the military, since my family has always been against it because I came from a communist country—Nicaragua. Well, my first choice was the Navy, so I set an appointment with the recruiter and he never showed up or called, so I said screw him. So the very same day the Marine recruiter called me so I set up an appointment with him for the next day and he showed up, so I decided to go with them. I've always liked responsible and reliable people because I was brought up under that with my parents, my dad especially. But mainly I thought about the military because I knew I wasn't college material.

b. What's was the most difficult thing or event you had to cope with during your first enlistment and why?

I only did one four-year term, but if I had to pick one thing that I had to cope with being a Marine was how sharp and squared away they were; they are overall unlike the other branches.

c. What was the easiest thing or event you coped with during your first enlistment and why?

Nothing is easy in life, but to me it was the whole discipline fact since my dad, even though he dislikes the military, raised us with that regimental kind of way, in his own way, teaching us how to be respectful, responsible, and organized. So, because of him my life was easier in the military.

d. If you met a young adult today who was interested in joining the US Military and you had a few minutes of their attention, what words of wisdom or advice would you give them?

I would tell them to make sure that's what he or she wants because the military could be the greatest thing but also could be your worst nightmare if you go in for the wrong reasons. Also, I would recommend them to at least graduate from college and go in as an officer. Not that is bad to go in as an enlisted, but we all know as an officer life gets easier, especially money-wise.

e. How long did you serve and in what branch?

I served from July 1998 to July 2002. USMC.

f. If you had to do it all over what would you have done differently while serving in the military?

The only thing I would change would be nothing but staying my ass in and making a career out of it, but a bad answer from my career planner and a bad choice on my part made me get out and move on from the military, but I really loved it all.

g. What do you do now for a living?

Ever since I left the service, I've been a local truck driver. Currently I'm still a truck driver working for the USPS since October 2017.

h. In what city do you reside?

Miramar, Florida.

Rollie Anderson, US Navy

a. How did you come up with the idea to enlist in the military?

While still attending high school, I knew that my parents could not afford to pay for higher education for me. So, I decided to join the United States Navy. Initially I signed a four-year contract and twenty-four years later, the rest is history. I can honestly say it was the best decision I have made in my life. The military helped me grow in ways I know any college education at that time would not have done. It made me into the man that I am today. Oh yeah, even after serving twenty-four years in this man's Navy I still was able to get my college degree.

b. What was the most difficult thing or event you had to cope with during your first enlistment and why?

My first enlistment was very difficult for me to deal with due to the deployments and getting fully acclimated to the military way of life. Yes, boot camp gives you the basics for being in the military, but it is a different story once a young man finally arrives at their first duty station and starts to deal with the everyday rigors of military culture. To be honest, I thought I was going to have a nervous breakdown. After my first three years I grew to understand the ways of the military, and as the years passed I was able to recognize that in all young military personnel I encountered, and I was able to coach them through that first enlistment transition. I guess we all went through it.

c. What was the easiest thing or event you coped with during your first enlistment and why?

The hard work and being a good follower. I had no problems with following orders and being attentive to what I was being taught or trained on. Hard work and dedication to work helped me get through the hard times during my first enlistment.

d. If you met a young adult today who was interested in joining the US military and you had a few minutes of their attention, what words of wisdom or advice would you give them?

I would tell them it is one of the best organizations to be a part of. It will help you see who you really are as a person. To be honest, the military is not for everyone, but the organization has done wonders for millions of young men and women who have had the great fortune of serving in the United States Military.

e. How long did you serve and in what branch?

I served for twenty-four years in the Navy.

f. If you had to do it all over, what would you have done differently while serving in the military, if anything?

I would not change a thing. I enjoyed my time in the service; there's nothing like it in the world. I was exposed to people, cultures, and countries that I would have never been exposed to if I had not joined the military. The main theme of my retirement was how the United States Navy helped me become a man, and during my tenure I hope I did enough to make the military as strong an organization as when I initially enlisted through doing the right thing and training the people that I came in contact with to carry on a great tradition.

g. What do you do now for a living?

I work for the United States Postal Service.

h. In what city do you reside?

Coral Springs, Florida.

Edwin Lopez, US Navy

a. How did you come up with the idea to enlist in the military?

I enlisted in the military in order to take advantage of the GI Bill benefits they were offering at the time.

b. What was the most difficult thing or event you had to cope with during your first enlistment and why?

The physical training aspect of basic training was the hardest. Why? Because I was out of shape when I got there. But I forged onwards and made it through. Also, being away from home (at that time the extremely laid-back environs of western Puerto Rico) for an extended period for the first time was pretty difficult.

c. What was the easiest thing or event you coped with during your first enlistment and why?

Traveling to places such as the Mediterranean, places I otherwise would not have had the opportunity to visit had I not been in the military, proved to be somewhat enjoyable, especially when shared with new friends.

d. If you met a young adult today who was interested in joining the US military and you had a few minutes of their attention, what words of wisdom or advice would you give them?

Make sure you get in shape BEFORE entering Basic Training! I would definitely encourage them to consider making a career out of it, since the early age at which the military affords retirement leaves ample time in which to go to school and embark upon a more lucrative second career.

e. How long did you serve and in what branch?

I served for four years as a member of the United States Navy.

f. If you had to do it all over what would you have done differently while serving in the military if anything?

I would want to serve as a Commissioned Officer.

g. What do you do now for a living?

I work for the United States Postal Service.

h. In what city do you reside?

Sunrise, Florida.

Mario A. Larin, US Marine

a. How did you come up with the idea to enlist in the military?

At a young age, I would see the commercials of the United States Marine Corps on TV and I would tell my mother, I will be one of them someday. After high school, in 2007, the idea that started at a young age by seeing those commercials came true. I enlisted in the United States Marine Corps.

b. What was the most difficult thing or event you had to cope with during your first enlistment and why?

I would say that the most difficult thing was the moving around from boot camp, combat training, MOS school, and first duty station. I wasn't used to moving around like that.

c. What was the easiest thing or event you coped with during your first enlistment and why?

The easiest thing was adapting to my first duty station. The Marines in the unit made me feel welcomed.

d. If you met a young adult today who was interested in joining the US military and you had a few minutes of their attention, what words of wisdom or advice would you give them?

I would tell them that the military is not for everyone and to do it for the right reasons. It is very demanding, but no matter what branch of service they choose to go into, the experience is like no other in life, and the people they will meet during their time in service will forever be family.

e. How long did you serve and in what branch?

I served for ten years in the United States Marine Corps.

f. If you had to do it all over, what would you have done differently while serving in the military, if anything?

I would make some different decisions.

g. What do you do now for a living?

I'm an IT specialist.

h. In what city do you reside?

Miami, FL.

Maria S. Morales, US Army

a. How did you come up with the idea to enlist in the military?

I had children early; I didn't have a sense of direction in which path I wanted to take. Ultimately, I joined to find myself.

b. What was the most difficult thing or event you had to cope with during your first enlistment and why?

Being apart from my family for long periods of time. I was obligated to leave my family to be able to provide for my family.

c. What was the easiest thing or event you coped with during your first enlistment and why?

Being exposed to a variety of people. Growing up, I lived amongst people with similar mind frames and in the military, you get to meet people with different cultures and upbringings.

d. If you met a young adult today who was interested in joining the US military and you had a few minutes of their attention, what words of wisdom or advice would you give them?

Continue your education while serving.

e. How long did you serve and in what branch?

Twelve years, Army.

f. If you had to do it all over, what would you have done differently while serving in the military, if anything?

I would've achieved at least a bachelor's degree.

g. What do you do now for a living?

City Carrier for the United States Post Office.

h. In what city do you reside?

Coral Springs.

Orlando Andujar, US Marine

a. How did you come up with the idea to enlist in the military?

I was seventeen years old in 1983 when we lost 241 Marines in a bomb attack in Beirut, Lebanon. During that time, I was receiving letters from my cousin Miguel who was stationed in Beirut and was among the handful of Marines who survived that bombing attack. When that day happened, I wanted to sign up for the Marine Corps, but I was a junior in high school and had one year left to graduate. I continued to correspond with Miguel, and when he came home on leave, he helped me sign up to be a US Marine. I arrived at Parris Island recruit depot, South Carolina on the stroke of midnight July 4, 1984.

b. What was the most difficult thing or event you had to cope with during your first enlistment and why?

One of my more difficult moments in the Marine Corps was the first time I drove a twenty-six-ton Amtrak (amphibious troop carrier) off the California coast and into the Pacific Ocean. I drove into the water hoping that I would not sink straight down into the ocean. Needless to say, the Amtrak did its job and once I opened the hatch and drove around the ocean for a while, I realized

I could do this job. Coming back onto land was at an angle, not a straight shot; I had to steer the Amtrak back onto land, bringing it in so as to not let the waves flip the carrier over.

c. What was the easiest thing or event you coped with during your first enlistment and why?

One of the easiest things I did was running. My training for wrestling and cross-country running in my senior year of high school helped me get in some shape.

d. If you met a young adult today who was interested in joining the US military and you had a few minutes of their attention, what words of wisdom or advice would you give them?

I would tell a young adult today who was entering the military to take things one day at a time and learn to follow orders and stay out of trouble in the service.

e. How long did you serve and in what branch?

I served three years in the Marine Corps.

f. If you had to do it all over, what would you have done differently while serving in the military, if anything?

If I had to do it all over again, I probably would have tried to be an officer in the Marine Corps.

g. What do you do now for a living?

I work in the recycling business.

h. In what city do you reside?

I reside in Morrisville, Pennsylvania.

CHAPTER 4

THE PROS

Leadership

You will learn how to lead people in a professional environment while learning new leadership skills. These are invaluable skills that will serve you well for the rest of your life. It's like having excellent people skills on steroids. Just think about that one boss, teacher, or family member in your life, that person you respect for their knowledge, personality, grace under pressure, and ability to motivate you and others. Don't confuse this with the comedian in your life. I am talking about the person who doesn't make decisions for you but simply gives you honest feedback that teaches you how to think for yourself.

You can't just walk into a store and say, "I'll have one can of leadership, please, the large can." Leadership is something that you learn over time. Without realizing it, you are observing other people leading and learning a little bit from everyone. This could be on the job, out with friends, or at home around family members. You pick a little something from all these people and slowly become a leader with your own style.

As your time in the military goes by, you will learn leadership while also getting promoted up the ranks. Shortly you will be responsible for accomplishing a job (mission) with a small group of people you are responsible for. As time passes you will improve your ability to speak in public and you will learn to tackle daily challenges. Your group of subordinates and responsibilities will grow tremendously.

These leadership skills will continue to grow and provide you with other opportunities in the military. If one day you decide to finish your enlistment and move on to the civilian sector, you will be highly qualified to lead people to success.

You will learn that as a veteran you will be more qualified to take on managerial positions in the civilian world than your nonveteran counterparts. Your ability to communicate effectively to motivate a group of people to get a job done will be easily recognized.

Here are a few examples of things I learned about leadership over the years:

I learned a lot of leadership through observation. I remember as a young Marine observing a much older Marine, a gunnery sergeant (E-7), running with us in formation one morning. I could tell he was not feeling well. He looked like he had the flu or at least a very bad cold. It was about 5:00 a.m. It was a cold North Carolina morning and there he was, leading us in a four-mile formation run chanting all those songs you see in military movies. I was nineteen years old and he was easily in his forties, yet he was leading us, without saying he was sick. He didn't complain about the weather. He said the cold rain is Marine Corps sunshine. He smiled, ran, and sang cadence the whole time. I could tell he wanted to lead by example. I also didn't want to be the one to drop out of that run.

Praise is a great form of leadership. I remember years ago, I must have been in the Marine Corps for about two years at the time, we had an individual-effort battalion-size five-mile run. I came in first in the battalion. I remember the colonel calling me to the side and asking me for my name. He then said, "Marine, you sure as hell can run fast, great job." Later I learned that he had been running on my heels all the time and was known for being a great marathoner. Looking back on it, I understand he could have passed me easily anytime he wanted. But he wanted *me* to be successful that day.

A Marine was late for work once and he was called in to see the sergeant. When he came out of the office everyone asked him what happened in the office. He just stood quietly and then commenced to work. After that he was late a couple more times and was asked to see the sergeant again. After the third visit we knew for sure he was in real trouble. Years later, I ran into this Marine who now was a sergeant himself. He said the sergeant back then wouldn't write him up officially for his tardiness but instead put him on guard duty during his weekends. He said the sergeant believed in him and didn't want to ruin his career. The sergeant was right; years later this Marine kept going up the ranks to eventually retire successfully.

Although it is hard to summarize leadership skills in a neat chapter, what I can tell you is that the civilian world is taking notice and realizing now more than ever how valuable veterans are to their bottom line. They realize that they save money and time by hiring veterans who are disciplined self-starters with goal-oriented personalities.

Friendships and Bonds

You will meet and make lifetime friends. There is a special camaraderie amongst military personnel that is difficult to explain to someone who hasn't finished at least one enlistment. Most of what you learn in the service will be learned from your peers. Depending on how you were raised, some of the things you learn will only magnify what your parents or siblings taught you. Other times, you will find father figures who will take you under their wings to teach you and guide you in the right direction.

Say you want to change the oil in your car; you have the money, the tools, and the base hobby shop, but you don't know how to do it. Now you'll have plenty of peers who would love to show off their skills and teach you how to do it. This is just one scenario that might take place on a military base. Most people don't know that some of our military bases are cities within a city, some with more than fifty thousand military personnel stationed and/or living there.

If you don't know something or you need to improve on a skill, there will always be someone available to teach you and help you, whether it be balancing a checkbook for the first time or cooking a small meal. The senior enlisted and officer ranks want you to be successful, because if you are successful in your military and personal life, then the unit you are now a part of will accomplish their mission continuously. Everyone on the base is away from home working; some, like you, are away from home for the first time.

Learning about Yourself

You will discover yourself through a challenging military life. The best way to explain this word *challenging* is by providing you with an example. It's Friday afternoon and you and your new military friends have the weekend off. You are invited to run a 10k race the next morning, but the farthest you have ever run is maybe four miles. You say yes and Saturday morning you run the 10k race (6.2 miles) with your friends and do exceptionally well. You just learned not only that you can run 10k, but that you actually like running and want to do it again.

One day during lunch you look over at your friend and you ask, "Hey, what are you reading there?" Your friend says, "Oh, I'm reviewing this paper I had to write for school." You learn that your friend is taking college courses after work. After some discussion you learn from your friend about the process of signing up for and taking classes on base. Before this, college might have been something on the back burner, not so important. But after you saw how your friend was chipping away at his degree path, your attitude about the college might have changed. Okay, maybe you won't decide to go to school because of one encounter. But after continuous exposure to most of your friends taking college courses either online or on the base, you may just decide to use this benefit of tuition assistance and get started on your degree. Remember, you are who you hang out with.

Educational Benefits

Tuition Assistance Program (TAP)

Use the tuition assistance program while on active duty and

take college courses in the evenings at no cost to you. Most military bases offer courses both on and off base or online. There is plenty of literature at the base education centers to get you started.

The key is to stop procrastinating. Take one class at a time and before you know it, you're on the stage graduating.

Forever Montgomery GI Bill

The military has an educational benefit called the GI Bill. These are educational benefits that you earn upon honorable discharge from the military. If you didn't finish your degree while in the military, you can use the GI Bill to finish. The Montgomery GI Bill is constantly being updated to meet the needs of our everchanging workforce and technologies. For example, when I joined the military the internet didn't exist. Today as a veteran you can take online courses and have them paid for by the Montgomery GI Bill.

College Funds

Sometimes, as part of your enlistment contract if you qualify, you could be awarded a college fund. These are extra monies to complement your GI Bill. After you have taken your ASVAB test, ask your recruiter about the qualifications for a college fund and if any are available.

I would emphasize that going to college is totally up to you. No one is going to force you to go. I took classes here and there. It was many years later that I decided to finish and earn my degree. During my last three years in the Marine Corps I used a tuition assistance program, and during my first year in retirement I used the Montgomery GI Bill to finish and earn my bachelor's. I did it on my terms and when I wanted.

Folks pursue a college degree for different reasons. I did it for two reasons: self-improvement and to be a role model for my children.

Travel

You can travel within the United States and overseas at little to no cost most times, unless you're on personal vacations. Within my first year in the Marine Corps at the ripe old age of nineteen, I had travelled to Norway, France, Scotland, and England. No, I didn't get there by air; I got there on an aircraft carrier, the *USS Iwo Jima*. Before this I had never been to sea.

During my second enlistment I traveled to and worked in Bogota, Colombia; Beirut, Lebanon; Izmir, Turkey; Kinshasa, Zaire (known as the Republic of the Congo today) and Montevideo, Uruguay.

During my twenty-five-year career I lived and worked in many cities both in the United States and abroad. I learned about many cultures and customs traveling to and living in South America, Africa, Europe, and some Caribbean islands. All this travel was a tremendous education.

The longer you serve, the more you will get to travel. I volunteered to go to many of these places. I know of some military members who didn't travel much at all and spent most of their careers on one base. It's a personal choice. I chose to travel as much as I could and learn as much as I could. I decided that knowledge was never going to be a burden to me.

Broaden Your Horizons and Learn New Things

You will meet people from all walks of life. During my time in the Marine Corps I made friends with people from across America. The experience of simply driving from North Carolina to Ashland, Kentucky for a Thanksgiving dinner with a fellow Marine was great and unforgettable.

Driving from North Carolina to California to a communications school, while the Marine Corps paid for my miles traveled, lodging, and food was in itself a great experience. At that time, I had never traveled across the United States coast to coast, especially driving.

Before joining the Marine Corps, my music selection was mostly in the Spanish language, salsa, merengue, and maybe a little soft rock. Today if you listen to my iPod (yes, I still own one) or read my playlist on iTunes you couldn't place me in any nationality with certainty. I have broadened my horizons beyond anything I expected. I learned to not only listen to but also enjoy a wide variety of music.

In all of my platoons in the Marine Corps there were Marines from a variety of cultural and financial backgrounds who all had different interest and hobbies. I learned a lot from them all. For example, early in 1982 I learned a little bit about photography from a Marine who owned a very fancy camera and was very knowledgeable. In 1983 I learned about freshwater fishing from a fellow Marine. In 1989 I learned about computers and saltwater fishing from Marines stationed with me in Guantanamo Bay, Cuba. I remember purchasing my second computer, a Tandy 1000SL, and learning from a Marine how to use it.

I could go on and on, but you must understand that you are who you hang out with. If you decide to join the military, remember to learn from your new friends and always help each other out. Your military tours and travels will be more enjoyable when you can share knowledge and kindness.

No Layoff

During my career in the Marine Corps, I always had a steady income, receiving a pay check on the first and fifteenth of every month. It wasn't uncommon during the ups and downs of the economy to hear of friends and family members losing their jobs and having to start again somewhere else. This no-layoff benefit allows you to plan and save for your future.

At the time of writing, the government has shut down over the battle to build a wall between Mexico and the United States. My military retirement check was deposited with no issues. It's good to know that when you retire successfully, a government shutdown is not going to directly financially impact you.

Learn a Trade

Learn a trade and get experience so you can land a great career after the military. Some people just do one enlistment and use the military as a stepping stone toward a career in the civilian world. There are many programs that encourage employers to hire veterans. Hiring veterans is smart business. If you're an employer and you hire a veteran who was honorably discharged, you're getting an employee who is physically fit, drug free, disciplined, and self-motivated. On average, veterans have a much better chance of being hired than nonveterans.

While in the military you have to be willing to learn new things. I have always believed that knowledge is power. Learning a trade is not just learning the trade that you were trained to do. You should also be learning the trades of everyone you work with and/or encounter while in the military.

I am going to age myself by saying that when I first joined the Marine Corps, administrative clerks were using Smith Corona typewriters. I watched as a young Marine could answer questions while also typing without looking down at the keys. I was impressed and told myself I wanted to be able to do that too. I purchased a book and basically taught myself how to type. To this day this skill has helped me tremendously.

Marines who are trained in the infantry fields usually move into law enforcement upon discharge. Marines in aviation fields spend a lot of time in training and are typically offered reenlistment bonuses. Every military occupational specialty (MOS) will present you with opportunities upon separation from the military.

Thirty Days Annual Paid Vacation

You will earn $2\frac{1}{2}$ days paid vacation for every month you work. You must know that although you may have earned the vacation days, there will be times that due to military operational commitments you will be denied a vacation. During most of my military career I was either able to take Christmas or New Year's vacation but not both. That's the part many people get stuck on; they don't understand the commitment that is required to keep this country safe. I can remember standing guard duty on many holidays and long weekends. I remember missing out on many birthdays and family events. I don't regret it; I just point it out so you remember that neither the Marine Corps nor any other branch of service can promise you every day is going to be a great one.

Most civilian companies now start you with two weeks' vacation; it will be years before you earn your way to four weeks' paid vacation a year. Just to be clear, you get paid while you're on vacation. What you pay for is the actual vacation: travel, entertainment, and food.

Health and Dental Care

The rising cost of health insurance won't be a factor during your time in the military. Before your discharge from the military, regardless of whether you served four years or thirty, you will be given a physical exam, including dental, to clear you for discharge. During my enlistments, every time I was transferring to another base for either school or work, I was required to be cleared medically with a complete exam.

If you decide to stay in the military and then retire, you will receive the tremendous benefit of low-cost, high-quality health and dental insurance. At the time of writing, as a military retiree I pay $49.50 monthly for my family health insurance and about $120 for our family dental insurance.

Tax-Free Room and Board

You will have an opportunity to save money because you don't pay for rent or food (free room and board). Out of your pay you can pay into a Thrift Savings Plan (TSP), which is a retirement account that you can start making withdrawals from at the age of 59½. Military personnel also pay into social security. Upon full retirement you will have multiple sources of income: military retirement, social security, TSP, and any other savings or investments you place in your retirement portfolio.

Just like going to college while in the military, no one is going to force you to save your money, but saving money while in the military is an opportunity you should learn to take advantage of.

I can't speak for all the military branches, but I can tell you that the Marine Corps provided me with a lot of training in financial planning. These classes were given to me at every leadership school I attended.

Special Pay

While you are in the military you will receive increases in pay for a variety of reasons: promotion, another year of service, cost-of-living adjustments, doing a special duty, or gaining special qualifications. Military recruiting is considered special duty. All recruiters get a monthly special pay just for being on recruiting duty and, no, it has nothing to do with how many people recruiters enlist. No military branch pays commission per enlistments. The pay amounts to about an additional $450 a month. This extra pay is because recruiters spend many hours working with applicants, parents, and educators. If you are required to use a foreign language during the performance of your duties, you can earn language proficiency pay. Or if you are in a jump status and your job requires you to jump out of planes (yes, with a parachute), you will qualify for these extra monthly monies.

Retirement Plan

People who decide to make the military their career are known as lifers. When you retire successfully from the military you will be provided with health insurance and dental insurance at a very reasonable price, as mentioned previously.

The military has a great retirement plan that works as follows: You complete a minimum of twenty years of honorable service and in return you earn 50 percent of your yearly basic pay for life, in the form of a monthly annuity. This monthly payment begins the very next month following retirement. Here is a basic example: A soldier is earning $48,000 a year in basic pay, so upon retirement after twenty years of honorable service he will receive $24,000. If you divide that sum into twelve months, his monthly retirement annuity will be $2,000 minus taxes, for life, with a cost of living increase as adjusted by the government from time to time. Not to complicate the math too much, but for every year over the twenty years of service, you earn another 2.5 percent in military retirement pay, up to a maximum of 75 percent for thirty years of service.

Aside from monetary benefits, another retirement benefit is your permanent military identification card that allows you to visit any United States military base in and out of the country. You can purchase merchandise at the military exchange and not pay taxes on what you buy.

Military Discounts

Many businesses and events give a military discount for products and/or services. I have personally used this benefit for many years while in the military and now as a retiree. I save 10 percent at Home Depot and Lowes all the time. I am not ashamed of using a benefit I earned. I thank all the businesses that extend their thanks and generosity to us.

CHAPTER 5

THE CONS

Leaving Home

You will leave home and work and live many miles away from your parents, siblings, and friends. From time to time as military operations may dictate, you will be completely out of touch with your family. Unfortunately, I got to a point where I couldn't tell you what my siblings were doing for fun. It's not that I forgot them; I just got so busy with learning and traveling that I sometimes lost touch for months at a time.

Military life takes a toll on long-distance relationships, and most don't last. There really isn't a nice way to put this one. Sometimes a young person talks about getting married immediately upon graduating from boot camp. I always recommended against that. Being married in the military is difficult, especially if you're new to the military and at a low rank. I didn't get married until I had served fourteen years, and I am still married today probably because of that decision to wait a little.

It is difficult to leave home, mom, and apple pie behind when you're young. I am sure you have heard the saying, "It is lonely at the top." I think this saying applies especially to the military.

Many of you will leave friends and family members for very long periods of times. When you return home, you will have little in common with most of your old friends. You will have become a different person with different goals in mind. This doesn't make you better or worse, just different.

Changing Your Lifestyle Completely

You may be sharing a room (bachelor-enlisted quarters) with one or two other military people as you go through initial training and once you start working in the military within your Military Occupation Specialty (MOS). Your living quarters will improve as you earn rank (get promoted). You need to know that you will be living in close quarters many times with strangers.

The Pay is Low

At least at first until you start to climb through the ranks. Although it was many years ago, I still remember my first paycheck was $265 every two weeks. Although I knew that the pay wasn't going to be great, it was still a shock to receive so little. Today the pay is much higher but still not up to cost-of-living standards. To emphasize how things change, when I first enlisted in 1979, on paydays I stood in a long line to receive cash, whereas today it is all done by direct deposit.

Military Grooming Standards

You will lose all your hair and have to follow a strict dress code during your enlistment, including maintaining a short haircut. This is not a big deal for most people, but it's good to know.

When not on duty in the Marine Corps you are required to wear a belt with your trousers and a collared shirt tucked in. Each service has their individual dress code standards.

You Could Die in Training or in Combat

You're joining the military to learn how to fight and defend your country. Let's not sugarcoat it; it may very well cost you your life. You could, just like your predecessors, find yourself in grave danger of serious bodily injury and/or death.

You Might Hate Your Job

You could find yourself doing a job you hate for four to six years, depending on the length of your enlistment contract. During my time in the Marine Corps I met people who absolutely loved the life of a Marine. I also met some Marines who were always miserable. They just didn't like what they got themselves into. Most completed their enlistments and immediately sought employment elsewhere. These people had calendars counting the years, months, and days until their contracts were up. I admired both their integrity and their commitment to finish their contract under honorable conditions.

Uniform Code of Military Justice (UCMJ)

Most people that enlist in the military have never heard of the UCMJ. After all, they don't enlist with the intention of getting in trouble with the law.

The UCMJ is what defines the military justice system. I list it as a con because if you are thinking about joining the military, you need to know everything you can about it. So, let me give you a scenario. You join up and after you have been in the military about a year, you show up late to work. The sergeant sits down with you and tells you this is unacceptable. Three days later you show up late again; now you are sent to see a senior enlisted member, such as a sergeant major, and he tells you that being late twice means he may have to take disciplinary action against you. He tells you that you need to get your act together and think about your military career. The third time you're late, you are what is known as "written up." So, you go to what is known as "office hours." Now the commanding officer reads the charges against you and hands you your punishment, which is commensurate with your violations. Being late to work three times may bring you no pay for one month and thirty days restriction to bachelor-enlisted quarters. This is just one example of how the UCMJ can affect you and your military career.

In all my years of service I never had anything to do with the UCMJ. My only involvement was as a chaser (a duty that involved escorting Marines to court martials and then to the brig). It is important for you to know that if you commit a crime in the civilian world you will be dealt with in your military branch also.

Here's an example: You get pulled over for driving under the influence on a Friday night. You and your unit were supposed to leave the next day aboard a ship for military exercises in the Mediterranean. When the unit holds roll call, you are not present because you spent the night in jail. You will be charged by the military for being on unauthorized absence (UA). You will also be charged with missing a movement—your unit has had to go on a military operation without you. Getting promoted up the ranks has just become very difficult, which will affect your ability to reenlist and stay in the military, if that was your goal.

I will say that most military members will never be impacted by the UCMJ; they joined the military to better themselves and they don't break the law.

CHAPTER 6

MILITARY RECRUITERS

The first and most important thing to understand is that the United States has an all-volunteer force. At the time of writing, no one is being drafted.

All military recruiters go through training in their respective services. Marine recruiters go to recruiters' school in San Diego, California for training, where they learn everything about recruiting. They are taught the do's and don'ts on how to communicate with potential applicants, educators, community leaders, and anyone they may encounter in the streets of America.

What Do Recruiters Do?

Recruiters are taught to prospect for qualified applicants. What this means is that recruiters are trained to visit places where young adults learn, work, and live in order to speak to them about opportunities in the military. Such places might be high schools, community colleges, universities, malls, and any other public place where young adults congregate.

Recruiters are taught to screen applicants for possible qualification or disqualification from military service. They are taught to screen for the three major qualifying categories:

educational status, physical fitness, and police involvement.

Recruiters are taught sales skills with an emphasis on interactive listening skills. This training helps recruiters present military benefits to applicants in a manner that is easily understood. These recruiters have already spent some time in the military, including boot camp, MOS school, and working in their respective fields. When they are recruiting in the streets of America, they are recruiting for all fields in their military branch, not specifically for the field they are in.

As a Marine recruiter, I clearly had a contracting mission but also a responsibility to all those I recruited. As I was, some of the kids I enlisted were intrigued by the challenge of earning the title of United States Marine. The way I spoke to young adults about their decision to join was as follows:

"Okay, I understand that you want to enlist in the Marine Corps. I further understand that you have been found prequalified. You have passed the Armed Services Vocational Battery Aptitude test, and you have no physical problems that would prevent you from passing our medical exam. You also don't have any issues past or present with police authorities. What I need you to understand is that I can only give you what you qualify for based on your ASVAB test scores."

As a recruiter I always informed my applicants that they shouldn't join the Marine Corps for the benefits, because the benefits are not enough of a motivator to get you through the challenges you are going to face in boot camp and the Marine Corps. What will get you through boot camp is the idea that you expected it to be challenging and your "can do" attitude.

I further explained to applicants that benefits are like awards and medals: If you rate them, the Marine Corps will get them to you. You don't have to chase them; they should chase you. As stated earlier, it is up to you to use your benefits and improve your life.

Story Time

A police officer at a restaurant says to the waitress while looking at the menu, "How are the steaks here?" The waitress responds, "Fair." The officer says, "That wasn't exactly a ringing endorsement." The waitress responds, "You looking for ringing endorsements or how the steaks are?" The officer smiles and orders something else. He understands this is a no-nonsense waitress who is not going to tell him what he wants to hear.

I need you to understand that a good recruiter will not paint a rosy picture about boot camp or military life. A good recruiter will not tell you just what you want to hear.

I am not demonizing someone who wants to join the military in order to use the benefit of educational opportunities such as tuition assistance and the Montgomery GI Bill. What I am saying is that the challenge and opportunity to serve your country should always override the benefits package.

A military recruiter contracting mission is just that—a mission. All military branches have their contracting and shipping missions. These missions are passed down to the recruiters with specificity such as how many high school seniors, graduates, females, and musicians we need to recruit. All large institutions have goals and mission statements.

Story Time

On a hot summer afternoon while working in South Florida as a recruiter instructor, I was asked to model for a recruiter who was having difficulties getting a parental consent. On the way to the home, the recruiter was telling me how difficult it was going to be. I listened to everything he had to say and then asked one question: "How does your kid feel about the Marines?" The recruiter replied, "Oh he definitely wants to join, his mom is okay with it, but his father is going to be a problem. When we get there, we have to wait a couple of minutes until his father get home from work." I say it is okay to wait and get to know the mom.

When the father arrived, he was polite, cordial, and had many questions. After I answered all his questions, he said to me, "Aren't you guys on a quota? You know, like you have to recruit so many people per month." I said, "Yes, we have a quota." I could see my young recruiter with a quizzical look on his face, and it appeared as though he was sinking deeper into the couch; maybe I imagined it. I asked the father, "How many hours did you work today?" "Eight hours," he said quickly. "Why not six or seven hours?" I asked. "That's the contract I signed for," was his reply.

Basically, my conversation with him was to point out that we are all held to some kind of quota or standard. I charge my recruiters to find me three of the best applicants monthly to enlist. If they only find one or two, no one is going to get fired. You see, these are just goals. Sometimes recruiters will find five, six, or more monthly. But I pointed out to the father two things. One, that it was his fault I was in his home to enlist his son, because he raised him properly and that meant his son was well qualified to enlist in the Marines. And two, that just because someone has a quota doesn't mean they are a bad person with bad intentions.

He and his wife signed the parental consent, and my recruiter was in shock all the way back to the recruiting office. His exact words were, "Top, I don't know if I can do that, you know, talk to people that way." I had a good coaching conversation with him, helping him understand that enlisting people in the military is an honorable profession. You don't lie or sugarcoat things. The more you love your branch of the military, the easier recruiting will come to you. This recruiter continued to recruit and successfully finished his recruiting tour.

Although military recruiters are taught to sell and persuade applicants to enlist, I believe that everyone who joins does so of their own free will. Directly or indirectly, I am responsible for the enlistment of hundreds of young men and women into the Marine Corps. I have never done anything in my lifetime more rewarding. I know I made positive changes in the lives of many.

I also spoke with and had full interviews with many highly qualified applicants who *did not* go forward with enlistment after my interview. I like to think that I treated every one of these people with respect and dignity before and after their decision. I also hope that they found their way in life and are blessed with great health and happiness. I don't believe you have to join a branch of the military to be successful. You can be successful regardless of your career path. I believed then and still believe that treating people the way you want to be treated will bring you success. Since retiring fifteen years ago, I have run into many of my recruits and I am happy to say that they are all successful today.

Now that you have come to your decision as to why you want to join (and again, people decide to enlist for different reasons), it's time to get organized and prepared for enlistment.

CHAPTER 7

WHAT QUALIFICATIONS DO YOU NEED?

Regardless of where you are in your life, when you decide that you are going to join the US military, there are a few things across all military branches that are the same. These are the qualifying categories that you must meet.

Citizenship

You must be a US citizen or legal immigrant (in possession of a green card), permanently residing in the United States.

Education

You must be at least a high school graduate or high school senior in good standing to graduate on time. You must the pass the Armed Services Vocational Aptitude Battery (ASVAB) test. The ASVAB is a three-hour test comparable to the SAT. This test is free. Some high schools across the country allow the military to give this test to hundreds of high school students at a time. And if you're a high school senior, you may use your passing scores to enlist. If you are seriously interested in joining the military and your high school is offering this test,

I highly encourage you to take it. At the very least it would be nice for you to familiarize yourself with the test and learn what you need to improve on for a better score another day. Test scores are good for two years. After enlisting, your scores are good for as long as you stay in the military.

There is one thing to understand about the ASVAB: The better your scores on the ASVAB, the more enlistment programs you may qualify for. If you barely passed the test, the military recruiter will only be able to offer you limited programs toward your enlistment. An example of this would be that if you scored low in the area of mechanical comprehension, chances are you are not going to qualify for an aviation mechanic job.

Your score will determine not only what programs you qualify for but also when you can ship to boot camp. If you have a sincere interest in improving your scores, visit a bookstore or purchase online an ASVAB study guide. These study guides have sample questions and exams. While writing this chapter I quickly found and installed an ASVAB app on my cell phone. I tested the app and found it to be very easy to use. There are many apps available for download that have practice multiple-choice questions broken down by ASVAB sections and also contain one or more sample tests to practice.

A high school student who has completed Algebra I, Algebra II, and Geometry and has good grades will have a great chance at scoring well on the ASVAB. Students who do well in English and read frequently will also do well. ASVAB results usually reflect a student's high school academic achievements.

Whenever I met a high school freshman who was really interested in the military, I would guide them by telling them exactly what they must achieve in the next four years of school to find themselves exceptionally qualified for military service. Are you trying to guess what I said to them? Guess no more; this is the advice I told any young freshman:

First and foremost, come to school prepared to soak up all the knowledge you can. Take all your classes very seriously and ask all the questions you want; make your teachers earn their pay. Your goal in each class is to crush it. To get the best grade in the classroom. Don't come to school with a goal of simply passing. Any fool can pass and earn a diploma. Your goal is all A's. An occasional B is acceptable. A C is not good; this means you can't C your teacher; you're blind. Make sure that you take all your required classes for a diploma and then some extra. Take classes in the summer to get ahead. Get all your math, English, and science classes done early.

While you are crushing school, slowly work your body into shape. Get clearance from your doctor for you to exercise. Start nice and slow; you are a freshman and have time to build great cardio, strength, and endurance.

Police Involvement

Your history of police involvement will bring your hopes for enlistment to an immediate stop or delay it or require you to apply for a moral waiver, if available. We all make mistakes, some larger than others. Some applicants assume that the problems they had with the law disqualifies them from ever enlisting, so they disqualify themselves and never speak to a recruiter, but that isn't necessarily the case.

As a Marine recruiter I encountered many young adults who had made mistakes in their life. Most of them I was able to help and enlist. Some I had to look straight in the eyes and tell them that I was sorry but the Marine Corps wouldn't look past their particular history and enlist them, so they were disqualified from enlisting. Let's look at an example to further explain. Let say that you score very high on the ASVAB, you are a high school graduate, and you're in great physical shape. But when you were fifteen you stole a car, went for a joy ride, and got busted with a charge of grand theft auto. You paid some fines, did some community hours, and spent time on probation. Now you're nineteen years old and in the past four years you have had no problems with law enforcement.

A good recruiter will present your case to his or her recruiting commanding officer for consideration for what is known as a moral waiver. If the waiver is approved, you will be able to enlist with some conditions. You may be required to ship to boot camp within thirty days and you won't be afforded the opportunity to enter some Military Occupation Specialties (MOS). For example, you would not become military police, military intelligence, and/or aviation mechanic. Basically, the military wants to enlist America's best people to defend her. Gone are the days when a judge will tell you to either go to jail for your crime or enlist in the military. Every branch of the service handles waivers differently.

Physical Fitness

You must be able to pass a complete head-to-toe physical examination at the Military Entrance Processing Station (MEPS). Every military branch has height and weight standards. There are some medical problems that will disqualify you from entering the military.

When you and a recruiter meet for the first time, the recruiter will ask you many questions about your health. They will ask you about your history of surgeries or hospital visits, and any allergies you may have. They will ask if you about any pins or metals that may have been installed. They will be very thorough when asking about any visits to a mental health professional.

The purpose for these questions about your health history is to disqualify you. Yes, you read that correctly; the recruiter is trying to save your time and theirs. It is the recruiter's responsibility to ensure they don't enlist anyone who is physically disqualified. Remember that your answers may not necessarily disqualify you.

If you are found to be mentally and morally prequalified but your answers about your physical qualifications are not encouraging or lead to more questions, the recruiter will require you to provide all medical documentation, which will be sent to the local Military Entrance Processing Station (MEPS) doctor for review. Usually within a few days the recruiting station will receive a response saying either the applicant can continue with enlistment, or the same MEPS doctor may say he will examine the applicant and then possibly send them to a local specialist. Note: These doctor visits to MEPS and referrals to a specialist are free of charge to the applicant.

The recruiter should always weigh you in the office and note your weight and height. Some applicants are overweight and at that moment will be disqualified by the recruiter. If you are mentally and morally qualified and find yourself physically disqualified because of your weight, please see your physician before embarking on a diet and exercise program.

Some branches of the military have some exercises that you must be able to perform before they will consider you for enlistment. The Marine Corps requires that you run a mile and a half, do some pull-ups and/or chin-ups, and some crunches/sit-ups. Again, please remember that requirements change from time to time. Check with your recruiter to learn of the current requirements.

The idea is to have you in decent shape as a starting point to begin a light physical training regimen, *before* you depart for boot camp. The better shape you are in, the easier things will be for you at boot camp. Recovery is the key word: The better shape you are in, the faster you will recover from physical training in boot camp. A good recruiter will teach you how to properly stretch and hydrate before, during, and after exercise.

I can't resist mentioning that in order to get better at pull-ups, you must *do* pull-ups. In order to get better at running you *must* run, and run on a physical path not a machine.

CHAPTER 8

AFTER ENLISTMENT AND BEFORE BOOT CAMP

So, yesterday you were at MEPS where you took your physical exam and then raised your right hand and swore in. Now you are in what is called the delayed entry program. You are still a high school senior, and your ship date for boot camp is three weeks after high school graduation, which is six months away.

Your recruiter will provide you with some information on certain exercises and may also take you to exercise from time to time. But because the recruiter is busy with continuous recruitment of young people like you, I am telling you to invest as much time as you can into getting yourself in great physical shape. You must have the discipline to do it yourself.

I enlisted in the delayed entry program in March and shipped out five months later in August. I felt both good and a little afraid that I was going to Marine boot camp in Parris Island, South Carolina smack in the middle of the summer. The feeling-good part was because I knew what I would be doing for the next four years. The afraid part was because maybe I really didn't know what I was getting into.

What was clear was that I needed to get into better shape.

All through grade school, middle school, and high school I attended gym class as a requirement in New York. The problem was, I weighed only 105 pounds and was five feet, four inches tall (okay, short). Today I am five feet three; my doctor says everything goes down as you get older.

I started to jog slowly, adding a little distance every two weeks to my runs. By the time I shipped out I could easily run three miles or jog four miles with no discomfort. I was doing push-ups and sit-ups daily, gradually increasing the numbers. By the time it came time to ship I could easily do fourteen pull-ups, about one hundred push-ups, and eighty sit-ups.

Most recruiters will make some time to train with you at least once a month. I only saw my recruiter three times: the day he picked me up to take me to my physical and enlistment at the MEPS in Philadelphia, once to exercise, and finally when he picked me up at home when it was time for me to ship to Parris Island. At the time I wasn't mad at him. After all, he never promised to get me into shape. It was explained to me that it was my responsibility to get prepared. It was a different time in our country; I am of the opinion that public schools today don't make a big deal of physical fitness unless you are on a sports team.

So, let's review some of the things you must do prior to your departure to boot camp. This advice applies regardless of which branch of the military you join.

First, you obviously passed the MEPS doctor's physical exam, so now you must **start a slow progressive exercise and proper diet program**. Start slow, take notes, and gradually increase your running distance. If available to you, go to a swimming pool and practice treading water (never alone in the water) for long periods of time. If you are slightly overweight, gradually decrease your food intake. Stop eating fatty foods and sweets. **Eliminate soda and candy and instead eat whole-wheat bread, nuts, fruits, and vegetables**. Your body is like an engine; it will only perform as well as you take care of it.

While taking care of your body with proper diet and exercise, **learn how to rest**. What I mean is stop hanging out late at night with your friends; they are not going to get you through the rigors of boot camp. Practice sleeping at least seven to eight hours of sleep each night. No, you didn't read that wrong. I did say, "Learn how to rest and sleep."

Learn how to hydrate. Some people have no problem drinking water. Others don't drink it and instead attempt to survive on juice and soda. You must immediately start drinking water daily. This is important because in boot camp you will be exercising a lot and drinking many canteens of water every day. How much? Divide your body weight by two and drink that amount in ounces. Today I weigh about 160 pounds, which means I should drink about eighty ounces of water daily. The best time to drink water is just before meals. Wait about five minutes for your water to digest properly, then slowly eat your meal. You will find that you will naturally eat less because you feel full with the water.

Very yellow urine means you are not hydrated; pale yellow is the goal. The clearer your urine, the better hydrated you are. Caution: Don't go crazy just drinking tons of water all at once. Drink your water slowly throughout your day. Everything you do to prepare for boot camp should be done slowly and progressively.

Along with taking care of your body, you must also **get your finances organized** before leaving town. So, pay everybody off and/or make arrangements to pay them when you return. But don't burn any bridges at home. You must be responsible for your personal life so that it doesn't follow you to boot camp.

Unlike when I enlisted, when there was no internet (don't laugh), you have the resources at your fingertips to **learn as much as you can about the military branch you just joined**. There is a lot of knowledge you should learn before you report for boot camp, to make life easier for you. After your enlistment your recruiter should have provided you with a pamphlet or flyers with information that you should study prior to arriving at boot camp.

When I enlisted, a small book was provided to me so I could learn about the Marine Corps before arriving at Parris Island. I learned Marine Corps Traits and Principles, my eleven general orders, customs and courtesies, and military language and/or jargon. Some examples of the jargon: the bathroom is called the head, the floor is the deck, and the wall is the bulkhead. All this knowledge was great to have learned prior to arriving in boot camp. The more knowledge you have and the better shape you are in, the easier life will go for you in boot camp.

Before arriving at your boot camp for the branch of service you joined, you have to make arrangements to **store your personal items**, including any automobiles or cycles you own. Your recruiter is not responsible for this.

Take the names and addresses of anyone you want to stay in contact with during boot camp. Yes, it's time to return to letter mail; you won't have your cell phone in boot camp.

CHAPTER 9

SUCCEEDING AT BOOT CAMP

All the military branches in the United States military have a boot camp. They may call it something else, but it will be a boot camp and a challenge both mentally and physically for most people.

I reported to boot camp weighing 105 pounds and obviously not very muscular. I concentrated on not the entire three months but on making it from meal to meal. I did the very best I could to listen to instructions and follow them from the time I woke up to breakfast. Then from breakfast to lunch. From lunch to dinner. From dinner until sleep time.

Many people who go through boot camp unfortunately exaggerate when they tell their story to a friend or family member upon returning home. These exaggerations tend to discourage a lot of people from joining the military.

Will boot camp be difficult? Yes, absolutely. The less you physically prepared, the harder time you will have. And, yes, some people do get sent home without completing boot camp. In the Marine Corps boot camp, if you get injured you get recycled, which means you won't graduate with your platoon. You will receive medical treatment and upon getting better return to training and eventually graduate.

My recommendations for success at boot camp are these:

- Listen and learn everything right the first time around. Learn from the mistakes of others.

- Don't daydream about home; concentrate on what is in front of you.

- Don't assume that because you haven't done something before, you can't learn it.

- Don't try to take short cuts or cheat your way to success. In other words, don't try to reinvent the wheel. You are going to be taught to do things in a certain way in a certain order. Just follow instructions; the methods being used are proven methods.

- Don't take things personally. The drill instructor doesn't know you and therefore doesn't dislike you. Their job is to test you both mentally and physically until just before your breaking point.

Anyone who has decided to join the military must also understand that this means they have also decided to drastically improve their physical fitness. So, to recap, what you need to do to prepare for boot camp are these things:

- Gradually get yourself in shape, with proper exercise and food choices.

- Learn how to hydrate yourself slowly; drink water.

- Learn how to rest your body by sleeping seven to eight hours a night.

- Get your finances in shape and pay off any debts before leaving for boot camp.

- Make arrangements to store your personal items, such as an automobile or cycle, etc.

CHAPTER 10

YOUR FIRST ENLISTMENT

Upon graduating from boot camp, you normally go home for about ten days of leave (vacation). In your possession you will have written military orders that state when and where to report for duty. Some people will be reporting to the military occupational school, while others will report directly to their military units. If you are reporting to a military unit you will be trained on the job in your specialty until a class starts.

Your first enlistment is your most difficult because you are new and have to adjust to military life while away from home. As you get to know people and the area where you are stationed, things will become easier for you.

My recommendations to you as a new military member are to be patient and give yourself time to adjust. Save as much money as you can, so that when you are afforded the opportunity to go on leave (vacation) you have the means to go home and enjoy yourself.

I also recommend that you find the base gym and continue to improve your physical condition. The better physical shape you are in, the easier military life will be for you. By the way, working out in the base gym is free. And, yes, free is my favorite word.

Each branch of the military has a branch of Morale Welfare and Recreation (MWR). They have many activities both on and off base that you and your family can participate in for free or at a discounted price. They have a calendar of events for you to choose from. Read the bulletin boards posted all over the base and you will be amazed by all the things you can do and learn.

Take the time to stay in contact with your family back home. I am a firm believer that if you forget where you came from, you probably don't know where you're going. I personally made it a point to call home two or three times a month. I used to call collect and then send money home to pay the bill. Then technology changed; I used all the technologies to stay in touch with friends and family. I also sent home gifts and souvenirs from my trips abroad.

I believe that the people who raised you and helped you along the way deserve not to be forgotten. You joined the military to improve your life and learn new things. Don't abandon your family; it's a bridge you will have to cross again one day.

CHAPTER 11

DECISION TIME: REENLIST OR MOVE ON?

Whether your first enlistment is for three, four, or six years, upon completion you may be interested on either reenlisting for more years of service or moving on to the civilian sector.

For me it was a difficult decision. I realized that after finishing four years I had not accomplished everything I set out to do. I reenlisted and did much better in my second enlistment. I became a Marine Security guard overseas, working with diplomats, making a lot more money, and saving a lot more. I took Marine Corps correspondence courses that were mailed to me. Remember, this was all before the internet. I also got in much better physical condition.

Once I finished my second enlistment and had been on active duty for seven years, it was easier to continue reenlisting. My new goal was to earn a retirement at an early age.

The decision to reenlist or move on should not be taken lightly. Only you, the service member, can decide which way to go. You just have to balance the pros and cons of your decision.

I would strongly suggest that if you discover during your first enlistment that you hate military life, have a plan to complete your enlistment honorably. Do this while getting as much college work done as possible while also saving most of your pay. I would also suggest that you send out resumes at least two to three months before being honorably discharged.

If you land a job with the government after your military service, you can use the military buyback program. This program allows honorably discharged veterans to add their years of military service to their years of civil service with their new government job. This will increase their retirement annuity when it comes time to retire.

Using the military as a stepping stone toward your success is not a bad idea. I enlisted quite a few Marines who after one enlistment moved on and today are very successful. Plan for your own success and take action to move forward with your life.

CHAPTER 12

A FINAL NOTE

Thank you for taking the time to read this book. I believe my intentions for writing it are good. I sincerely want anyone thinking about joining any branch of the military to do their due diligence and do some research.

Remember, if you decide to join, it will be challenging and you need to decide how successful you want to be. The military is not just a workplace; it's a game changer. You must get up and give it your all every day.

The military is an honorable profession. I take my hat off to all those who made the ultimate sacrifice so that we can live in freedom.

God bless America.

ABOUT THE AUTHOR

Miguel A Nieves was born in Utuado, Puerto Rico and raised in Brooklyn, New York. Upon graduating from high school in 1979 he joined the Marine Corps and reported to Marine Corps Recruit Depot, Parris Island, South Carolina for boot camp. He served for twenty-five years and four days active duty (but who's counting?) and retired a Master Sergeant of Marines.

Some of his duties and assignments included Wireman; Wire Chief as member of Beirut, Lebanon Multinational Peacekeeping Force; Marine Security Guard (MSG Duty), Kinshasa, Zaire and Montevideo, Uruguay; Barracks Duty, Guantanamo Bay, Cuba; Marine Recruiter; Recruiter Instructor; and District Contact Team member for recruiting.

He was awarded the Meritorious Service Medal, Navy Commendation Medal 3rd award, Navy Achievement Medal 2nd award, and Good Conduct Medal 8th award.

He graduated from American Military University with a Bachelor of Arts in marketing, and he currently resides in South Florida.

Made in the USA
Lexington, KY
12 December 2019

58384663R00061